Teen Voices
Real Teens Discuss
Real Problems™

Teens Talk About
Learning
Disabilities
and Differences

Edited by Jennifer Landau

Featuring Q&As with Teen Health & Wellness's Dr. Jan

Rosen
YA™
New York

Published in 2018 by The Rosen Publishing Group, Inc.
29 East 21st Street, New York, NY 10010

First Edition

Library of Congress Cataloging-in-Publication Data

Names: Landau, Jennifer, 1961– editor.
Title: Teens talk about learning disabilities and differences / edited by Jennifer Landau.
Description: New York : Rosen Publishing, 2018. | Series: Teen voices : real teens discuss real problems | Includes bibliographical references and index. | Audience: Grades 7–12.
Identifiers: LCCN 2017019686| ISBN 9781508176527 (library bound) | ISBN 9781508176602 (pbk.) | ISBN 9781508176367 (6 pack)
Subjects: LCSH: Learning disabilities—Juvenile literature. | Teenagers with mental disabilities—Education—Juvenile literature. | Teenagers with mental disabilities—Biography—Juvenile literature.
Classification: LCC LC4704 .T43 2018 | DDC 371.9—dc23
LC record available at https://lccn.loc.gov/2017019686

Manufactured in China

The content in this title has been compiled from The Rosen Publishing Group's Teen Health & Wellness digital platform. Additional original content was provided by Barbara Gottfried Hollander.

Contents

4 Introduction

8 Chapter 1
Teens Talk About Attention Deficit Disorder

17 Chapter 2
Teens Talk About Dyslexia

33 Chapter 3
Teens Talk About Learning Differences

44 Chapter 4
Teens Talk About Asperger's Syndrome and Nonverbal Learning Disability

52 **The Teen Health & Wellness Personal Story Project**

53 **Glossary**

54 **For More Information**

57 **For Further Reading**

59 **Bibliography**

62 **Index**

Introduction

When you are young, you learn to speak, read, and write. Not everyone learns or does these things the same way. Some people speak with their voices; others with their hands or communication devices. When people read, they interpret letters that form words. Some people may interpret these letters incorrectly, which then translates into inaccurate sounds. Writing is another tool that can be done in many ways because it is a process that involves forming thoughts, organizing ideas, and then expressing those ideas.

The brain is a complex organ that performs these functions. It is composed of three parts: the brainstem, cerebellum, and cerebrum. The largest part of the brain, the cerebrum, has four lobes: frontal, parietal, temporal, and occipital. The frontal lobe is responsible for speaking and writing. The parietal lobe interprets language, and the temporal lobe of the brain decodes sounds.

How the brain functions affects learning. There are many ways to learn. Some people are auditory learners.

A participant at the St. Louis Augmentative and Alternative Communication Theater Camp uses a computer to rehearse his lines in the camp's play.

They learn best by listening. Others are more visual learners and acquire knowledge most effectively by seeing the material. Certain learning disorders further affect learning styles and the tools needed to succeed in academic environments. For example, a student with auditory processing disorder (APD) has difficulty distinguishing sounds used for words.

Other medical conditions can influence how students acquire, process, retain, and express information. For instance, attention-deficit/hyperactivity disorder

(ADHD) is a neurological condition that can make paying attention challenging. It is difficult to complete a reading assignment if you can't stay focused on the text. Dyslexia is another learning disorder that affects reading as well as language development. Learning disorders can also influence how students process math and written expression.

Some disorders affect communication and social abilities, which can hinder success in school.

Examples include Asperger's syndrome and nonverbal learning disability. Interacting with peers, including within the classroom learning environment, is an essential part of school. Having difficulties with reading social cues or understanding other people's feelings makes it hard for students to connect with their classmates. This can turn into a frustrating situation for students and affect learning, especially in group activities.

The left side of the brain is associated with logic, math, science, and language, while the right side is associated with intuition and artistic expression, such as the ability to play music.

Share Your Own Story

The stories you are about to read were submitted by your peers to the Teen Health & Wellness Personal Story Project. Sharing stories is a powerful way to connect with other people. By sharing your story, you can connect with others who are dealing with these challenges. Find more information about how to submit your own story at the end of this resource.

Once a learning disability is diagnosed, students and their support team, including family members, teachers, psychologists, and psychiatrists, can institute plans to achieve academic success. Sometimes students perform effectively in mainstream programs with support, such as aides or modified schoolwork. Other times, students may function more successfully in schools specifically designed for their learning disorders. With an effective game plan, students can learn successfully.

Chapter 1

Teens Talk About Attention Deficit Disorder

Attention deficit disorder, or ADD, is officially known as attention-deficit/hyperactivity disorder (ADHD). If you have ADHD, you could be mostly inattentive (lacking focus), mostly hyperactive (very active) and impulsive (prone to acting without planning), or a combination of all three. Having a combination of all three is the most common form of ADHD.

The attention process has three parts. Think about watching a video for a homework assignment. First, you decide to watch the video. Second, you focus your attention on the video. Third, you continue paying attention to the video to finish your assignment. If you have ADHD, you might be distractible, so active you can't sit still, or spontaneously decide to do something else in the middle of viewing. All of these things make doing homework very hard!

ADHD is a neurologically-based developmental disability. It can affect a person's behavior, moods, and cognitive abilities. For example, a person with ADHD may be constantly moving, talking too much,

Teens with ADHD often have trouble focusing on schoolwork. Therapy and medication can help those with ADHD function more effectively in their daily lives.

prone to interrupting, and unable to stay in her seat. She can have difficulty focusing, organizing activities, or remembering things. A person with ADHD can even exhibit anxiety, anger, low self-esteem, and mood swings.

Millions of children have ADHD, with this condition following them into adulthood. Diagnosis for this disorder is made by medical professionals using guidelines from the American Psychiatric Association's

People with ADHD may also suffer from anxiety, depression, or other mental health disorders. Having these additional disorders can make treatment more challenging.

Diagnostic and Statistical Manual, Fifth Edition (DSM-V). Treatments for ADHD include therapies like cognitive behavioral therapy (CBT), which seeks to modify a person's thoughts and behaviors in response to emotional distress. ADHD is often also treated with stimulants, such as Ritalin and Concerta, or cognition-enhancing medications, like Strattera and Intuniv.

Christi's Story

I was always the smart girl. The girl who sat in the back of the class and was done with her work before anyone else. I was also really shy and took a while to open up to people, but when I did open up everybody told me the same thing. Everyone said that I was going to be someone someday, maybe an author or an actress, just someone famous. Even if I was just the smart girl, I could always smile about that because I knew someday the other kids would look up to me.

Because I was ahead of my peers in a lot of things, it soon became apparent that I should be in advanced classes. I was so excited! Finally I could show off how smart I was. Finally I could do what I was really good at. By this time I was in fifth grade and things were super, super easy. My report cards were great, my parents were happy, and I was even getting to be a little less shy.

Then junior high school rolled around. By the time I was in seventh grade I was in every advanced subject that I could be in and took no regular classes. I knew going in that I had to be focused and keep my grades up. But suddenly things were changing. I traded in my T-shirts for "cute" clothes. My friends were no longer nerdy and smart, but theatrical and flirty. I had guy friends and got asked out a lot. This was all great except that my grades where slipping. In eighth grade I discovered my passion—theater. I was in a play, a musical, and two choirs, plus I played lacrosse. I was never home and still in really hard classes. That's when things got bad.

I couldn't pay attention to anything in school and I was daydreaming all the time. I wasn't the smart girl anymore; I was the girl who rushed to get her homework done when it was due in a few minutes. I was the girl who barely got by, and the girl who was always grounded. I was scared and anxious because I was always getting yelled at. Nobody believed I was trying at anything. They decided that I just didn't care. The scary part was that I did care. I cared a lot. I tried hard, but I just couldn't learn. Nothing was working. So I just

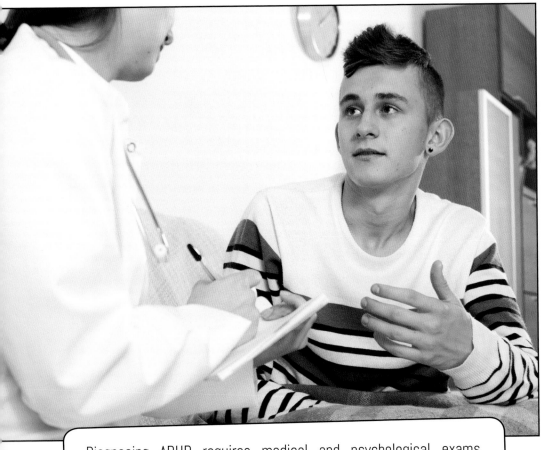

Diagnosing ADHD requires medical and psychological exams, including a complete medical history. Mental health professionals and primary care doctors can provide these types of diagnoses.

gave up. Things were too hard, and I was switching schools the next year to go to a private high school anyway, so I just decided to enjoy it while it lasted.

Unfortunately my parents didn't see things the way I did. In fact I was grounded from spring break until the Fourth of July. It was terrible. I felt like I was sinking, and that no matter how hard I fought there was no way out of failure. Then the answer to my prayers came: I was diagnosed with attention deficit disorder. This was bittersweet because I also felt a little embarrassed about it. And when I started freshman year I remember how hard it was to find the right medicine and dosage for me. But I'm proud to say with a lot of work I have turned things around. My GPA went from a 2.9 to a 3.8. I am doing really well in school, and I feel like I have that promising future back.

ADD can be scary; you can feel dumb and stupid. But trust me, things will get better. No one thinks I'm not smart any more (in fact quite the opposite). ADD is a real condition, and if you have it you need real help. It's not something to be embarrassed about. I'm just glad I took control of the problem before it really took control of me.

Tom's Story

I never understood what was wrong with me. Everyone else seemed to be doing fine. Why was I struggling? I couldn't read nearly as well as the other kids in my class. No matter how hard I tried, I never understood what was being taught.

It would take me hours to do my homework after school. I could never concentrate long enough to get it done quickly, and the smallest things distracted me. Whether it was a loose bolt on my chair, a fly on my lamp, or a car outside my window, I was distracted for three quarters of the time I was doing schoolwork. During the time that I could concentrate on my work, I moved at a snail's pace.

After this had gone on for a couple of years, my parents had me tested. It turns out that I had attention

Students with learning disorders may benefit from attending specialized schools. For example, the Shelton School in Dallas, Texas, provides educational opportunities for hundreds of students with learning differences.

deficit disorder and dyslexia. This explained why I had trouble concentrating and why I was struggling with reading. After I was diagnosed I started taking medication to counteract my ADD and I also started seeing a tutor, who helped my reading fluency. With this combination I was able to keep up with everyone else in my class.

I started to make better grades. But I still felt out of place. The tutor and the medication could only take me so far. I needed a place where I would be allowed to grow and where I could learn more easily.

My parents and I started looking for schools that fit the bill. After a few months of searching we landed on Shelton. It was a perfect match. So at the beginning of fifth grade I was enrolled in Shelton. I immediately felt at home. All of my teachers understood what I needed and were happy to oblige. If I needed help after class my teachers would go out of their way to make sure I got the attention I needed.

Looking back now as a senior, it's amazing to think that I have come so far. It has been challenging at times, but each of those challenges has taught me more about myself. And now as the school year is coming to an end, I'm heading off to college and can't wait for that next set of challenges.

MYTHS **AND** FACTS

MYTH   Only children and teens are diagnosed with ADHD.

FACT   Some people are in their twenties, thirties, and even sixties when first diagnosed with ADHD.

MYTH   ADHD is found only in boys.

FACT   Even though boys are diagnosed with ADHD twice as often, both boys and girls can have ADHD.

MYTH   ADHD is curable.

FACT   ADHD is manageable but not curable. It is a lifetime medical condition.

Chapter 2

Teens Talk About Dyslexia

Dyslexia is a common learning disorder, with over three million cases each year. The disorder is genetic, which means it is passed to family members through the genes. According to the International Dyslexia Association, dyslexia affects males and females almost equally. It also evenly impacts people of different ethnic and socioeconomic backgrounds. Because dyslexia influences reading and language processing, it is sometimes called a language-based learning disability.

People with dyslexia have difficulty reading. They struggle with decoding, or translating letters and words into speech. For example, people with dyslexia find it hard to match letters to sounds and to distinguish letter and syllable patterns. Other symptoms include difficulties with processing auditory information, understanding quickly administered instructions, managing time, learning new languages, and computing math and spelling

Having dyslexia can make teens feel frustrated, upset, or sad. They try to read, spell, and remember sounds and words, but their brains are processing

In Latin, dys means "difficult," while in Greek, lexia means "words." Dyslexia is a neurologically based learning disorder that affects a person's ability to read.

things differently. Teens with dyslexia may watch their friends reading quickly and wonder why it is so much harder for them. These teens worry about being called on in class and not being able to recall the right words. They may even have trouble with fine motor skills, like using zippers and buttons.

Children with dyslexia require individualized learning programs, instruction that may be easier to find in specialized schools. Occupational therapy and psychotherapy can also help with developing coping

The Individuals with Disabilities Education Act (IDEA) includes the required certification for special education teachers and individualized education programs (IEPs) with specific student goals.

tools, such as memory strategies for spelling and rhyming games for verbal expression, as well as ways to soothe feelings of frustration and anxiety. The skills gained early in life help dyslexic children grow into teens and adults with effective coping strategies. While dyslexia is a chronic disorder, people with this learning disorder can excel at academics, in the workplace, and in social settings.

Harper's Story

A Day

I have always thought it to be true that one's childhood foreshadows and defines one's future. The moments of childhood may later seem petty, trivial, and juvenile, but the things we do when we are young, with no regard for the world or its pressures, show our true, untainted intentions. My story is one I tell with confidence: one that I am happy to say defines me and shows who I really am beneath all the world has put on me.

It was third grade, and things seemed to be trucking along. There were no roadblocks and everything glowed with a childish simplicity. That was, until that day, that all-important watershed of a day. It was on that day that something inside me decided to write. Writing wasn't something I did often, if at all. Nonetheless, something within me moved me with the crazy idea of poetry. It was then that the simple poem "A Day" was born.

A day. A day.
A good day.
You can play on a day.
Day. Day.
What a day.
A fun day.
The day is gone.

I don't exactly remember sitting down at my elementary school desk and writing the poem, but I remember the emotions of the writing process. I can vividly imagine what it must have been like.

Sitting in the little navy chair, hunched over the dark, patterned wood of the desk, writing on a piece of notebook paper with a plain, semi-dull number two pencil. Reaching the third line and beginning to write, "You can play on—" Stopping, frustrated. Beginning to write the word "such," but not knowing how to finish it. "S"— a vigorous erasing. Again—"S" and a vigorous erasing. But I must have taken a deep breath and moved on. This kind of thing was normal.

I kept on writing, my hand probably beginning to cramp from my rough grip on the pencil and my inexperience with writing. All was going well, until the last line. The day is done, I must have thought as I wrote the beginning of the line. Yes, that's a perfect ending. But then, I stopped. My pencil hovered over the paper, my mind willing the correct spelling of "done" to come through, but it wouldn't. I couldn't figure out how to spell "done," so, with remorse, I ended the poem with "gone" instead and moved on to the illustration, because, after all, it was third grade and every third grade poem deserved an illustration.

I started with the tree, an apple tree, and then moved to the skinny strip of grass on the bottom and the yellow, youthfully drawn sun in the upper left corner. Next, the sky. I grabbed a blue marker and proceeded to color the whole piece of notebook paper blue. The remarkable thing that baffles me still to this day was that the marker, the old, blue Crayola marker, still worked like new for years after that, despite being run over the whole entire paper. That has to mean something, right? Surely that couldn't have just been a coincidence.

After writing "A Day," I was given a chance to read my poem to the class. I was thrilled, honored to get to share it. Before I took the floor, another girl read a short story she had written that day, and although I listened intently, her story wasn't nearly as good as I was sure my poem was.

I got up without a hint of nervousness and read my poem. In hindsight, I don't think anyone actually paid attention to me; they were third graders after all, and, honestly, how many third graders are literature enthusiasts? Nevertheless, I felt proud of my poem

and was content to just feel the words fall out of my mouth. After I had finished, my teacher said something I will never forget. "We have two kinds of writers in this class: authors and poets." That afternoon, I came home with a burning zeal for poetry. I wanted to teach my parents how to write a poem. I told my mom I wanted to put on a poetry school, and she said I could after she and my dad talked with me about something.

Dyslexia presents several challenges, such as difficulty reading aloud. People with this learning disorder may need to reread sentences several times to comprehend them.

This part, I remember clearly. We sat down on the couch. There was a strange imbalance in the air, and it brought out my nerves in a way I hadn't expected.

"Can you think back to second grade?" my mom asked, starting the conversation.

"Sure. Going back to second grade," I responded overenthusiastically, moving my hands as I spoke, both mannerisms [and] nervous ticks.

My mom proceeded to ask if I remembered a boy named Hunter. Of course I did. Hunter was a friend of mine, and no one in our class could forget when he was pulled out of class in the afternoons. I distinctly remember walking down the hallway with the class once and seeing Hunter watching a videotape about letters on one of those big, portable school TV sets in another classroom.

"Hunter had dyslexia," my mom must have said, although I do not recall the exact words she used.

The next thing she said was that I had dyslexia, too. I remember not exactly understanding what that meant for me, but understanding it enough to know that it must have been a bad thing. And in that moment, it was a bad thing, so I cried, but only because I felt I had to. How else was I supposed to react? I knew even then that dyslexia wasn't some deadly disease, but I felt I had to have some sort of reaction, so I cried and once the obligatory tears were all out, we talked, like the communicative family that we are.

Now, a good eight years later, my world has changed. I go to a different school, a private one for students with learning differences. I have different friends, friends that see me for who I am, and I am more than twice the age I was when I wrote "A Day." But despite all that, I am not a different person. Sure, I have grown, matured, and come a long way since "A Day," but I am still the girl I was when I wrote that simple poem. I am still the dyslexic writer who just wants to make people happy with her words, her writing.

It is no mistake that I was first called a writer and a dyslexic on the same day. The two are intertwined for me, and I am proud of both of them. There will never be a day where I am not dyslexic. That it just how it works. But that fact doesn't upset me—it brings me great pride.

Dyslexics are among the best thinkers, innovators, and dreamers of this world. Albert Einstein, Alexander Graham Bell, and Agatha Christie are all famous dyslexics and, with luck, some day my name will be added to that list. And why might I make such a list? Because I am a writer, a writer with big dreams, big stories, and big plans. I want to rule the world by sharing my world. Call me naive, but in the words of Steve Jobs, yet another dyslexic, "The people who are crazy enough to think they can change the world are the ones who do."

Brent's Story

Dyslexia has been the source of most of my problems in school. It slows me down in class, and it gets old having to work harder to get grades that most people can get without trying hard.

A person with dyslexia may require extra time to read and comprehend material. Visual strain can also be a challenge with reading and writing tasks, such as taking standardized exams.

In English class we read out loud. We go around in a circle taking turns reading. I am the slowest reader in every class. When I have to read out loud in class I become embarrassed. Everyone can tell that I am struggling, because I stumble over words. When it takes me a while to break down the word, people will read the word for me. I do not like this because that tells me they don't think I can read the word, but I can, I just need a little longer than normal. This also slows me down when I am completing a worksheet. I may have to read over the directions more than once to make it flow and make sense.

In my writing class we, of course, write many papers. Between being a poor reader and a worse speller my papers are choppy. I read over my writing, but I cannot catch all of my errors. So when I had to read my paper in front of the class it was embarrassing. Sometimes it did not make sense. I have learned to have a teacher read over my paper and make corrections before I read it to the class.

Having this learning difference has taught me that I must work hard to be successful at whatever I am doing. It has also taught me to have a good work ethic. Since it takes me longer to do an assignment, I must not wait until the last second to complete it. I do not think I would be where I am today if I did not have dyslexia. However, I do also wonder how my life would be different without it. I know I would at least not be at the same school.

I go to the Shelton School, in Dallas. It has taught me to be organized and be my own self-advocate. They have also taught me how to proofread my papers and not be scared to go and ask my teachers for help. I use the teachers so much some would be surprised if I did not come in for help every day.

Kevin's Story

So you are going to college with dyslexia. I'm not going to sugarcoat this message. You will face significant challenges, but with hard work (and some strategy), you can overcome them and triumph.

You Can Do College

I have dyslexia and school got easier the higher I got. Law school was easier than college; college was easier than high school; and high school was easier than grammar school. Grammar school was bad. Spelling tests every Friday were torture. Spelling in eighth grade was the last thing I ever failed. And once I got to college, I never got a grade below a B+.

So don't think, "Gee, I'm having trouble in high school. I could never handle college." That's nonsense! The "smart kids" in high school are those who can look at a page and memorize it, which dyslexics cannot do. I've had my current job for four years, and I still need to check my own business card to tell people my work phone number. In college, you can find majors where memorization doesn't count for much. (I did well in economics and highly recommend it.)

Don't Sweat the SATs

Don't be discouraged by your standardized test scores. SAT scores are not indicative of a dyslexic's true aptitude. Actually, I'm not sure standardized tests are a good measure of anyone's aptitude. I know lawyers who aced the LSAT, and I wouldn't hire them to represent my cat.

Consider Addressing Your Dyslexia Head On in Your College Application

In your college applications, consider writing an essay about your dyslexia. Talk about how it presents challenges, but in overcoming those challenges, you have gained a different perspective that others don't have. Such an essay has a number of advantages. It will make your application stand apart from others. You can always write more forcefully about something you feel strongly about (and I'm sure you feel strongly about overcoming dyslexia—I know I do).

Plus, it shows you have a diverse viewpoint, which you came to by overcoming adversity. A good essay on overcoming dyslexia will do a lot to make an admissions committee overlook less-than-stellar SAT scores.

Use Your Ears

If your dyslexia is like mine, it is a disorder of the "mind and the eye" but not of the ear. So I am in my element doing things orally (rather than in writing). Consider taking English courses that focus on drama (which involves the spoken word). Never cut class because you will remember much more of what you hear in class than what you see in a book. Choose professors who are good lecturers and participate in class discussion.

Use Technology

Type everything on a computer. Spell-check and auto correct are crucial for dyslexics. Voice recognition

Diagnosed with dyslexia, Mollie Schaefer could not read until the age of nine. In April 2017, Mollie became the University of Alabama's first Fulbright Scholar award winner.

software is getting better. And I'm told that there are great features on tablet PCs for dyslexics.

Work So Hard It Becomes a Habit

All that said, there are some things that are harder for us than for others. So just commit to working harder than the next guy. If you develop a good work ethic, you will find that your ability to work hard soon becomes an advantage that overwhelms the disadvantages of dyslexia. Many times my classmates or coworkers have said, "Gee, Kevin, I could never work as hard as you." In reality, they probably "could" work as hard as I do, but they "don't" work as hard as I do because they never learned how. My work habits are the best gift that my dyslexia has given me and a true competitive advantage.

Never Give Up

People will tell you that you cannot do things. They are small-minded and wrong. Ignore them, work harder, and leave them in your wake.

All the best,

Kevin

Kevin J. Kehoe Jr.
Microsoft Corporation
Senior Attorney (Antitrust)

Ask Dr. Jan

Dear Dr. Jan,
Since I moved I have experienced a lot of problems with friends. I figured out that my mom told some other moms about my mess and issues and ADHD. I was not pleased. Knowing now that everyone knows, I have a feeling the rest of my life is going to suck. I want to know how to get friends with them knowing and other parents knowing that I have ADHD, which is hard because your life revolves around ADHD and trying to fit in and school work. I have had trouble focusing, and now that I'm in high school it's even harder, especially with all the cool people and me being weird because I have ADHD. I need your help on how to get friends and stand up for myself.
— Mitchell

Dear Mitchell,

It sounds like you moved recently, which can be very tough, especially in high school. Hopefully, as you adapt to your new surroundings, you will find that it gets easier to adjust and make new friends. You also mention your difficulties with attention deficit hyperactivity disorder (ADHD). While ADHD can certainly be a huge challenge, you don't want to be defined by it. We all have strengths and weaknesses, including in the way that we learn. There are many learning difficulties, including ADHD, which can make school and life way more challenging. At the same time, it is important that we don't define who we are based on our challenges. You may also be surprised that most high school students secretly feel that they are weird, regardless of having learning problems like ADHD. Even though you have ADHD, it is important that you also identify and focus on your strengths. Maybe academics are really tough, but you're good at sports, or dancing, or art. It is important to maximize your opportunities to become involved in extracurricular activities where you can

(continued on the next page)

Ask Dr Jan

(continued from the previous page)

experience success and meet other teens that you can relate to better because of your shared interests.

I can understand your frustration with your mom telling other friends' moms about your issues. Hopefully, you were able to let your mom know that you would appreciate it if she were more respectful of your privacy in the future. Keep in mind, however, that you're making a lot of (hopefully false) assumptions about everyone knowing and the rest of your life sucking as a result. While we all worry, worrying usually just makes us anxious and is rarely helpful. So consider trying to not assume the worst, and make efforts to seek out friends who like you for who you really are. Ultimately, they're the only real friends worth having anyway.

If you focus on your strengths, accept the fact that you (like everyone else) have challenges, and seek out friends with common interests, it will be much easier for you to make friends and stand up for yourself.

Chapter 3

Teens Talk About Learning Differences

Children can have learning differences that affect how they acquire academic skills and complete learning-related activities. Individualized education plans (IEPs) describe a student's learning needs and provide guidance for addressing them within the educational system. Public schools provide special education services based on IEPs. There are also some private schools specifically designed for children requiring more specialized learning environments.

According to the Mayo Clinic, dyslexia, dysgraphia, dyscalculia, and nonverbal learning disability are the most common learning disorders. Dysgraphia impacts written expression, while dyscalculia influences how students learn and apply math. Symptoms for teens with dysgraphia include avoiding or not completing writing assignments, while teens with dyscalculia find it hard to do mental math, be on time, and compare amounts, such as scores for games.

There are several causes for learning difficulties, including genetics, medical issues such as exposure

Fine motor skills use small motor muscles to perform specific movements, like lifting and holding spoons or pencils. Some people with learning differences need help developing these skills.

to drugs and alcohol in the womb, and environmental factors such as exposure to lead. Child psychologists can aid in the diagnosis of learning disorders. Treatment plans may include additional learning resources, medication, and both speech and occupational therapy. For example, occupational therapists can help students with dysgraphia learn to hold pencils, trace objects, and use keyboards.

Auditory processing disorder (APD) also affects learning because it impacts how people understand speech. For instance, a person with APD may not be able to distinguish between similar sounds. APD cannot be cured, but it can be managed with the help of professionals, such as speech therapists, neurologists, and otolaryngologists, who are doctors who treat disorders of the ears, nose, and throat.

Stephanie's Story

A situation that changed my life was when I was diagnosed with learning differences. I was very young at the time, but I knew there was something not right with me. The person that did my testing was very nice and told me that I had dyslexia and auditory processing disorder. I had no idea what those differences were. My mom had to explain to me that I would have trouble learning to read and comprehend. She said that my auditory processing disorder would make me need to hear things more than once. I was still very confused.

We found a school made for children with learning differences. I am still at the school getting remediated and learning how to work through my challenges. I can live with my differences by finding other ways to help me read. I found that audio books that read the story to me help me comprehend what I read. At the school I attend, I have the ability to get the notes to make sure that I have everything I need to be successful in my work.

I learned that I can do anything I want, but it will just take a bit longer. I have the same intelligence, but I just learn and think differently. I learned that others would not judge me for not being up to speed. I am not alone in the work and will never be. There are many things that help boost my confidence: when I finish a book, no matter how long it takes. When I do well on an exam, I feel good that I was able to comprehend what I had learned and apply it to what I was being tested on.

My advice to other students is that you may be different, but you are special in your own way. Dealing with these issues can be very hard, but with the right support you can do anything. People need to learn that having learning differences should not hold you back from achieving your dreams. It is just another part of your story and may even make people respect your journey more. Keep a positive outlook on life, and let the cards fall where they may. You define your life, not your setback. As this quote from an anonymous author says, "Don't confuse your path with your destination. Just because it is stormy now, doesn't mean you aren't headed for sunshine." You will have rough patches in life and some may tell you they will never go away, but I was told I would never be able to go to college or make it through high school, yet here I am writing this paper as a senior, and I have not looked back.

Looking back on my past, I realize that I may not be the best at everything, but I have come pretty far. I was the kid that sat alone in the room because I did not want to be called on and say the wrong thing. I was—and still am—afraid of failure, but I learned if you use positive self-talk that it can and will help you in the long run. Even if you fail a test, if you know you did your best then you should still be proud.

Until I was a freshman school came easy to me. I was a straight-A student and was able to do all my work with ease. My first challenge, I was very scared. I had received my first bad grade, and it killed me to see it be put into the grade book. At that point I knew it was going to be a rocky road to graduation. As the year went on I found myself having subjects that I was really good at and some that were killing my GPA. By the end of the year, I was an A/B student. My parents were still proud that I made it through one year with those grades.

The next year, my learning differences came back to haunt me. I had a hard time in one class and couldn't

A student with learning differences who needs to take a standardized exam can prepare by studying practice exams and using breathing exercises to help reduce anxiety,

get over the hump. I would freak out whenever I had a test in the class. I had received my first C on my transcript, and I thought it was the end. I cried for days thinking that my life was over. My parents calmed me down and said that I had two more years till college and I had time to make that bad grade mean nothing.

Junior year came and it was the most stressful year of my life. I knew that this was the year that makes or breaks you. I did well at first and then I hit another rough patch. I managed to get through it and then I did really badly on my ACT. There, I thought, went my college opportunity. I took it again that summer and did better, but not good enough. Senior year came easily, but I got into college through summer school. I hated the idea of summer school and I still do. I hope that it works so I can go to nursing school and prove to myself and the world that my learning differences never held me back.

Julie's Story

I understood that my peers were not having the same difficulties in school as I was. They all seemed smarter and could complete the tasks that were asked of them super fast. As a young girl, I used to lie to my friends about my grades because they always got As and I always got a D or an F, no matter how hard I studied. Teachers would call on me to read in class, and I couldn't read a simple paragraph.

When I was starting off in elementary school, I noticed that I was reading slower than the other kids and having more trouble with the simple tasks that were asked of me. I would fail spelling tests and I couldn't do simple addition problems. I could never stay on task and was always getting left behind in a lesson. My parents started to see my difficulties with learning when teachers pointed out my grades and my lack of progress. They put me into the special ed program, which was so embarrassing. I was told to go get tested at an evaluation center to see what was going on. A few days after I was tested, I was told that I had learning differences, dyslexia, and ADD. At first I felt stupid and

Schools that specialize in learning differences can be a tremendous help to students who struggle in school. These schools offer the support and resources to help those students succeed.

wanted no one to know about my "disabilities." I kept up the lying to my friends and still wouldn't go get the help that I needed.

Pushing through junior high was rough: my grades were horrible, and I always just barely made it by. When high school came around, I was into the first semester when I finally had enough of struggling through my classes. I had to make one of the biggest decisions of my life: I wanted to go to Shelton, a school specifically for kids with high IQs who have learning differences. I knew making the transition would be difficult, as it would mean leaving my friends and social status. Although this change would be hard, I knew it was best for me.

I have been at Shelton for three years now, and my life has completely turned around. I am an A student and have been accepted to colleges that I never thought I would have the slightest chance of getting into. I have never been so proud of myself. I feel a sense of accomplishment and success, and now I can pursue my dreams.

Elizabeth's Story

"Come on, Elizabeth, I know you know this," were the words I continuously heard throughout the beginning of my high school career. And I did know it; I just couldn't figure out anything that was going on in class. Absolutely nothing made sense to me. My internal screams and cries for help melted my brain as if it was an iceberg steadily fading away. At that moment, I looked my future straight in the eye and discovered that

I was never going to be smart. I would live the rest of my life as the class blonde, the airhead, the one without any destiny.

Just two years ago, my entire life revolved around a prayer to be knowledgeable about anything. All I needed was a flick of light for inspiration. But nothing happened soon enough. My grades dropped significantly, and I had to begin the quest for my ideal college to attend (if I even graduated high school). Stress finally threw me off my mountain of life in 2006, and at the end of tenth

A teen with learning differences can find school a very frustrating place, but there are protections in place. The IDEA states that every student is entitled to a "free appropriate public education."

grade at Allen High School, I decided I was going to give up. I thought up plans of my future survival. Now looking back, tears come to my eyes.

The following summer was busy beyond belief. My family and I decided to move me to another school and one thing was for sure: I had to find teachers who understood me. My mother and I journeyed around the Dallas area in search of the perfect education for me. After plenty of disappointments, we came to our last option: the June Shelton School. I walked through the large, bare high school, gazing at photographs of teenagers just like me who had struggled immensely

WHO TO CALL

The following hotlines and organizations can offer support to teens dealing with issues related to learning disabilities and differences:

Council for Exceptional Children
(888) 232-7733
9 a.m. to 5 p.m., EST, Monday to Friday

Crisis Call Center
(800) 273-8255
Twenty-four hours a day, seven days a week

National Suicide Hotline
(800) 442-HOPE [4673]
Twenty-four hours a day, seven days a week

Thursday's Child Youth Advocacy Hotline
(800) USA-KIDS [872-5437]
Twenty-four hours a day, seven days a week

because of their learning differences. Their stories were posted on the snow-white walls and told how the discovery of their dream school had helped them achieve their potential.

After meeting with my dream school's principal, my hopes fell on the floor. My new life that I wanted so badly was completely out of our price range. I went home that day with an empty feeling of fear. I didn't know what else to do. I awoke the next morning to a large, colorful breakfast and rejoicing music in the breakfast room. My mother jumped out of nowhere and exclaimed that I was going to Shelton. I was going to make a difference, and I would graduate high school.

After facing endless trials at school, finding mentors who wanted to educate me felt like a dream come true, and turned my life around. When I look back now, I hurt for others who are like the girl that I was at my former school, and I pray that they will find their way.

Chapter 4

Teens Talk About Asperger's Syndrome and Nonverbal Learning Disability

Both Asperger's syndrome and nonverbal learning disability (NVLD) affect social skills. Asperger's syndrome is on the "high functioning" end of the autism spectrum disorder (ASD). While people with Asperger's have average or above-average intelligence and language development, they have difficulties in social situations and poor coordination. They struggle to read social cues, or signals based on body language, facial expressions, tone of voice, and personal space. People with nonverbal learning disability (NVLD) generally have very good verbal skills, but have challenges with social skills, visual-spatial skills (the ability to process where objects are located in space), and fine motor skills, like buttoning buttons or tying shoes.

Sometimes with these disorders, there is comorbidity, or the presence of more than one medical condition. For example, a child can have Asperger's syndrome or NVLD and sensory processing disorder. Symptoms for this disorder can include being afraid of loud noises, physical contact, crowds, and movement on playground and amusement park equipment. Having two disorders can make socializing even more difficult for a child. Both conditions can also negatively affect coordination and the ability to respect other people's physical boundaries.

Treatment for Asperger's syndrome or NVLD includes support groups and coping mechanisms such as

Bonding with other people is a basic human need. Teens on the autism spectrum have difficulty with socialization, which can cause them to feel isolated, angry, and depressed.

mindfulness to reduce other symptoms, like anxious thoughts. Mindfulness means being fully present without judgment. Its exercises promote better concentration, self-awareness, and reduced anxiety. These disorders are also addressed with individual and family therapies. These programs may consist of cognitive behavioral therapy (CBT), a talk therapy which seeks to change negative emotional responses that arise from psychological distress, and applied behavioral analysis (ABA), which rewards appropriate social responses with positive reinforcement. Modified learning plans or specialized schools can also provide more successful academic experiences.

Sierra's Story

My name is Sierra and I have Asperger's, autism, ADHD, and emotional problems. This is my story.

I don't know much about how I got it, but then again no one does; it just happens like that and it stays, but imagine how I felt learning I had each one of them, separately, one at a time.

I knew I had emotional issues when I was about four or five years old. After school, I had emotional breakdowns a lot of the time. I knew I was different, but I had no idea I had autism or ADHD until my parents told me that, and I got an individualized education plan (IEP). I always had problems paying attention, and I was falling behind in class so it wasn't until later that I realized I was different from the other kids. I started to wonder if it was good or bad.

I was in the fifth grade when I was taken to a doctor's office to get tested and there I learned I had Asperger's. In other words I had emotional problems, couldn't focus, was hyperactive, and autistic.

Taking care of those things is easier said than done. Focusing was the first thing I needed to take care of, so I take medication to help me. The other issues are much harder to deal with.

I needed someone to talk to about these problems, so I joined a group where everyone has issues in common. I was nervous the first time I went because I thought they wouldn't accept me. I simply told them about myself, and we all became good friends.

I needed a ton of help with schoolwork. Fortunately, one of my IEPs spells this out and I can get help with both school- and nonschool-related problems.

Having these issues has changed me as well. I no longer think that I am normal, and that is

Nathan Selove, a student with Asperger's syndrome, sits with his service dog in Nathan's Virginia high school. Service dogs can help teens become less anxious and more independent.

all good with me. I now think about acceptance. If you learn you have a disability, think about the bright side.

Stephanie's Story

There have been many ups and downs in my high school years, but if I had not found my voice and spoken up, I would not be here at the Shelton School. Throughout the years that I have been in school, I have always struggled with learning material—especially when it started to get harder.

Eventually, I was so unhappy with my academic struggle that it overflowed into my social life. Through all of elementary school, I mainly struggled with reading. Then, we moved to St. Louis when I started middle school. The material in sixth and seventh grade wasn't too bad, but when I got into eighth grade my struggle truly began. I was starting to really have trouble in math.

Meanwhile, I was always upset about something and my friends just couldn't take all the complaining and sadness anymore. In addition to those struggles, high school rolled around and made it worse! My teachers were not as willing to help me, and when they did I still didn't understand the material. And being me, I was too scared to ask questions and advocate for myself.

During my sophomore year, I really focused on math and not so much on my other subjects. I stayed after school twice a week and had a math tutor and still failed geometry the whole year. Working so hard without any so-called "pay off" was hard. I felt like I was failing at life. You could see that feeling written all over my face.

Then, my sophomore year social studies teacher, Mr. Good, saw that I was a bright, intelligent student but that I just couldn't put the pieces together while I was learning. He and my mom talked. Soon after that I was placed in a reading/study strategies class. Between my parents, my social studies teacher, and my reading teacher, they all knew I had a learning difference, but just didn't quite know what to do. I started going to a doctor once a week/every other week and he determined that I had nonverbal learning disorder.

Addressing learning disorders in an academic environment often requires a team that focuses on an individualized approach to students: individualized learning, progress, and success.

This is where the incredible Dana Feldman came into play. My mom was talking to her about my struggles and my diagnosis, and she said, "You have to come look at Shelton!" A week later, we interviewed and I was fortunate enough to get into the school. Signing the contracts was such a life-changing moment for me. My grades have gone from Cs and Ds to As and Bs just in the six months that I have been at Shelton.

All I can wonder is, what if I had never complained to my mom about how hard school was? What if I hadn't had Mr. Good as my US history teacher? What if I didn't have the determination and courage to follow through with school instead of giving up? What if my mom hadn't ever met the Feldmans? Without questioning something, there will always be a part of you that will be wondering. Wondering what is and what could be. Yes, I still have the same problem I have had my whole life, my learning difference. But my success here at Shelton is not because I have learning differences, but because I am being helped and not spoon-fed.

10 Great Questions
to Ask a Guidance Counselor

1. If I can't pay attention in class, does that mean I definitely have ADHD?

2. Who can determine if I have Asperger's syndrome?

3. What caused my learning disability?

4. How can I get an individualized learning plan (IEP)?

5. What provisions can be made to help me in school?

6. Where can I learn about schools that specialize in my learning disability?

7. Where can I find therapists to help me?

8. Will a medical professional treat my disability with medication?

9. What are the therapies most effective for my learning disorder?

10. Are there support or social groups to help me cope?

The Teen Health & Wellness Personal Story Project

Be part of the Teen Health & Wellness Personal Story Project and share your story about successfully dealing with or overcoming a challenge. If your story is accepted for online publication, it will be posted on the Teen Health & Wellness site and featured on its homepage. You will also receive a certificate of achievement from Rosen Publishing and a $25 gift certificate to Barnes & Noble or Chapters.

Sharing stories is a powerful way to connect with other people. By sharing your story, you can connect with others who are dealing with these challenges. Visit teenhealthandwellness.com/static/personalstoryproject to read other teens' stories and to submit your own.

Scan this QR code to go to the Personal Story Project homepage.

Glossary

anxiety Feelings of worry, restlessness, or nervousness about an unknown outcome.

audio Relating to sound, including its recording, interpreting, and broadcasting.

cognitive Having to do with the mental processes related to perceiving, remembering, and reasoning information.

coordination The organization of different parts to work together as an effective whole.

disability A mental or physical condition that results in limitations of senses or activities.

disorder An illness of the mind and/or body.

fine motor skills Movements that require the use of small muscles in body parts, such as fingers, toes, and wrists.

genetic Related to a unit of heredity called a gene.

neurologist A medical doctor that diagnoses and treats disorders of the nervous system.

psychotherapy Emotional-based treatment of a mental disorder.

self-esteem Confidence in oneself and one's abilities.

special education Instructional learning given to children with exceptional needs, such as students with learning disorders.

speech therapist A professional who helps people with speech, language, communication, and/or feeding challenges.

stimulant A medication aimed at helping increase focus and attention in children, teens, and adults with ADHD.

For More Information

The Asperger/Autism Network (AANE)
51 Water Street, Suite 206
Watertown, MA 02472
(617) 393 3824
Website: http://www.aane.org
Facebook: @AspergerSyndrome
AANE provides individuals, families, and professionals
    with educational material, support groups, programs,
    coaching, and means for advocacy.

Centers for Disease Control and Prevention (CDC)
1600 Clifton Road
Atlanta, GA 30329
(800) 232-4636
Website: https://www.cdc.gov
Facebook: @CDC
Twitter: @CDCgov
Instagram: @cdcgov
The CDC provides information about a wide range of
    disorders, including ADHD and autism. The CDC's
    website offers details on the diagnosis and treatment
    of these conditions, as well as statistics on their
    prevalence in the United States.

Council for Exceptional Children (CEC)
2900 Crystal Drive, Suite 1000
Arlington, VA 22202
(888) 232-7733
Website: http://www.cec.sped.org

Facebook: @cechq
Twitter: @CECMembership
The CEC seeks to provide optimal education outcomes for students with special needs.

Learning Disabilities Association of America (LDA)
4156 Library Road
Pittsburgh, PA 15234
(412) 341-1515
Website: https://ldaamerica.org
Facebook: @LDAAmerica
Twitter: @LDAofAmerica
LDA educates people about learning disabilities. Its mission is to help every individual with a learning disability fully participate in society.

Learning Disabilities Association of Canada (LDAC)
#20 – 2420 Bank Street
Ottawa, ON K1V 8S1
Canada
(613) 238-5721
Website: http://www.ldac-acta.ca
Facebook: @ldacacta
Twitter: @ldacacta
As a national nonprofit organization, LDAC works across Canada to promote equal opportunities for all people with disabilities. Its services include research, education, and awareness promotion.

Ontario Ministry of Education
14th Floor, Mowat Block
900 Bay Street
Toronto, ON M7A 1L2

Canada
(800) 387-5514
Website: http://www.edu.gov.on.ca/eng/parents/speced.
    html
Twitter: @ONeducation
This government department provides information on
    special education programs and services to help
    students succeed in academic environments.

Teen Health and Wellness
29 East 21st Street
New York, NY 10010
(877) 381-6649
Website: http://www.teenhealthandwellness.com
Teen Health & Wellness provides nonjudgmental,
    straightforward, curricular and self-help support on
    topics such as diseases, drugs and alcohol, nutrition,
    mental health, suicide and bullying, green living, and
    LGBTQ issues. Its free Teen Hotlines app provides a
    concise list of hotlines, help lines, and information
    lines on the subjects that affect teens most.

Websites

Because of the changing nature of internet links, Rosen
Publishing has developed an online list of websites
related to the subject of this book. This site is updated
regularly. Please use this link to access this list:

http://www.rosenlinks.com/TNV/Learn

For Further Reading

Cook O'Toole, Jennifer. *The Asperkid's (Secret) Book of Social Rules: The Handbook of Not-So-Obvious Social Guidelines for Tweens and Teens with Asperger Syndrome*. London, UK: Jessica Kingsley Publishers, 2013.

Eide, Brock L., and Fernette F. Eide. *The Dyslexic Advantage: Unlocking the Hidden Potential of the Dyslexic Brain*. New York, NY: Penguin Group, 2012.

Geffner, Donna. *Auditory Processing Disorders: Assessment, Management, and Treatment*. San Diego, CA: Plural Publishing, 2012.

Goldstein, Sam, and Nancy Mather. *Learning Disabilities and Challenging Behaviors: Using the Building Blocks Model to Guide Intervention and Classroom Management*. Baltimore, MD: Paul H. Brookes Publishing Co., 2015.

Grossberg, Blythe. *Asperger's Rules!: How to Make Sense of School and Friends*. Washington, DC: Magination Press, 2012.

Harris, Karen R., Steve Graham, and H. Lee Swanson. *Handbook of Learning Disabilities*. New York, NY: Guilford Press, 2013.

Holland, Jennifer L. *Train the Brain to Hear: Understanding and Treating Auditory Processing Disorder and Other Learning Disabilities.* Boca Raton, FL: Universal Publishers, 2014.

Lin, Y.S. *Defeating Depression* (Effective Survival Strategies). New York, NY: Rosen Publishing, 2016.

Nuttall James R., and Linda Nuttall. *Dyslexia and the iPad: Overcoming Dyslexia with Technology*. Seattle, WA: CreateSpace Independent Publishing Platform, 2013.

Porterfield, Jason. *Teen Stress and Anxiety* (Teen Mental Health). New York, NY: Rosen Publishing, 2014.

Reeve, Elizabeth, and Elizabeth Verdick. *The Survival Guide for Kids with Autism Spectrum Disorders*. Golden Valley, MN: Free Spirit Publishing, 2012.

Shea, Therese. *ADD and ADHD* (Teen Mental Health). New York, NY: Rosen Publishing, 2014.

Taylor, John F. *The Survival Guide for Kids with ADHD*. Golden Valley, MN: Free Spirit Publishing, 2013.

Bibliography

"Asperger Syndrome." Teen Health and Wellness. Rosen Publishing, November 2015. http://www.teenhealthandwellness.com/article/54/asperger-syndrome.

Autism Speaks. "Asperger Syndrome." 2017. https://www.autismspeaks.org/what-autism/asperger-syndrome.

Brain Balance Achievement Centers. "Sign and Symptoms of Sensory Processing Disorder." 2017. https://www.brainbalancecenters.com/blog/2012/04/signs-and-symptoms-of-sensory-processing-disorder.

"Brent's Story." Teen Health and Wellness. May 2016. http://www.teenhealthandwellness.com/article/141/11/brents-story.

Centers for Disease Control and Prevention. "Attention-Deficit/Hyperactivity Disorder (ADHD)." October 5, 2016. https://www.cdc.gov/ncbddd/adhd/diagnosis.html.

"Christi's Story." Teen Health and Wellness. October 2016. http://www.teenhealthandwellness.com/article/32/8/christis-story.

"Elizabeth's Story." Teen Health and Wellness. May 2016. http://www.teenhealthandwellness.com/article/141/12/elizabeths-story.

"Harper's Story." Teen Health and Wellness. May 2016. http://www.teenhealthandwellness.com/article/141/16/harpers-story.

International Dyslexia Association. "About Dyslexia: Frequently Asked Questions." 2017. https://dyslexiaida.org/frequently-asked-questions-2/.

"Julie's Story."Teen Health and Wellness. October 2016. http://www.teenhealthandwellness.com/article/32/10/julies-story.

"Kevin's Story." Teen Health and Wellness. May 2016. http://www.teenhealthandwellness.com/article/141/13/kevins-story.

Mayfield Brain & Spine. "Anatomy of the Brain." 2017. http://www.mayfieldclinic.com/PE-AnatBrain.htm.

Mayo Clinic. "Dyslexia." 2017. http://www.mayoclinic.org/diseases-conditions/dyslexia/basics/symptoms/con-20021904.

Mayo Clinic. "Learning Disorders: Know the Signs, How to Help." 2017. http://www.mayoclinic.org/healthy-lifestyle/childrens-health/in-depth/learning-disorders/art-20046105.

Optometrists Network. "Attention Deficit Disorder." 2017. http://www.add-adhd.org/ADHD_attention-deficit.html.

"Paul's Story." Teen Health and Wellness. May 2016. http://www.teenhealthandwellness.com/article/141/14/pauls-story.

"Sierra's Story." Teen Health and Wellness. November 2015. http://www.teenhealthandwellness.com/article/54/10/sierras-story.

"Stephanie's Story." Teen Health and Wellness. October 2016. http://www.teenhealthandwellness.com/article/32/9/stephanies-story.

"Stephanie's Story." Teen Health and Wellness. May
    2016. http://www.teenhealthandwellness.com
    /article/141/17/stephanies-story.
"Tom's Story." Teen Health and Wellness. October 2016.
    http://www.teenhealthandwellness.com/article/32/11
    /toms-story.
Walters Wright, Lexi. "4 Types of Social Cues."
    Understood for Learning and Attention Disorders,
    2017. https://www.understood.org/en/friends
    -feelings/common-challenges
    /picking-up-on-social-cues/4-types-of-social-cues.

Index

A

Asperger's syndrome, 6, 44, 45
  personal stories, 46
  treatment, 45, 46
attention deficit disorder (ADD), 8
  personal stories, 11, 13, 38
attention-deficit/hyperactivity disorder (ADHD), 5–6, 8–9, 10, 31
  diagnosis, 9–10
  myths and facts about, 16
  personal stories, 46
  treatments, 10
attention process, 8
auditory processing disorder (APD), 5, 34–35
autism spectrum disorder (ASD), 44
  personal stories, 46

B

brain, 4, 17
  function of, 4–5
  parts of, 4

C

communication devices, 4
coping strategies, 18, 19, 45

D

dyscalculia, 33
dysgraphia, 33
dyslexia, 6, 17–19, 33
  personal stories, 13, 20, 24, 26, 35, 38

G

genetics, 17, 33

H

hotlines, support, 42

I

individualized education plan (IEP), 33, 46
individualized learning programs, 18
International Dyslexia Association, 17

L

learning, types of, 4–5
learning differences, 33
    personal stories, 38, 40,
      48
    possible causes, 33–34
    treatment plans, 34
learning disabilities, 7, 17
learning disorders, 5, 6, 7,
      17, 19, 33, 34

N

nonverbal learning disability
      (NVLD), 6, 33, 44, 45
    personal stories, 48
    treatment, 45, 46

S

sensory processing
      disorder, 45
social cues, 6, 44
standardized tests, 27
support numbers, 42
support team, 7

T

Teen Health & Wellness
      Personal Story Project, 7

About the Editor

Jennifer Landau is an author and editor who has written about psychological bullying, cybercitizenship, and drug and alcohol abuse, among other topics. She has an MA in English from New York University and an MST in general and special education from Fordham University. Landau has taught writing to young children, teens, and seniors.

About Dr. Jan

Dr. Jan Hittelman, a licensed psychologist with over thirty years experience working with children and families, has authored monthly columns for the *Daily Camera,* Boulder Valley School District, and online for the Rosen Publishing Group. He is the founder of the Boulder Counseling Cooperative and the director of Boulder Psychological Services.

Photo Credits